An Alphabet In Five Acts

by Karen Born Andersen
Pictures by Flint Born

DIAL BOOKS ☀ NEW YORK

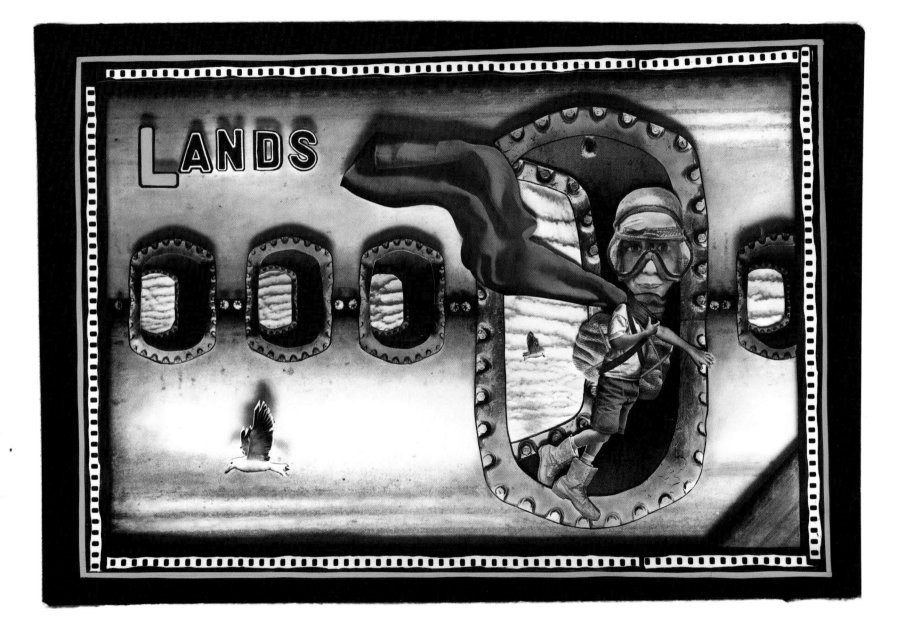

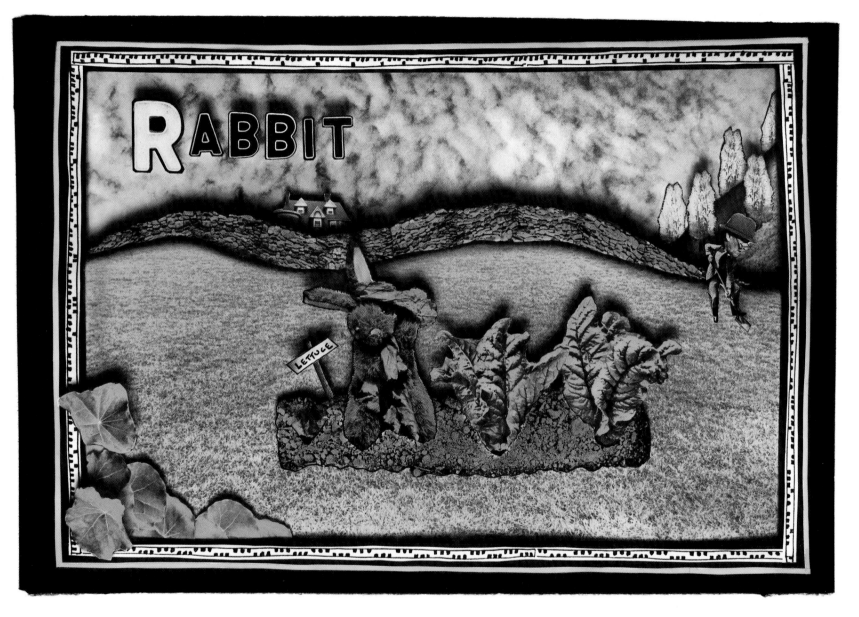

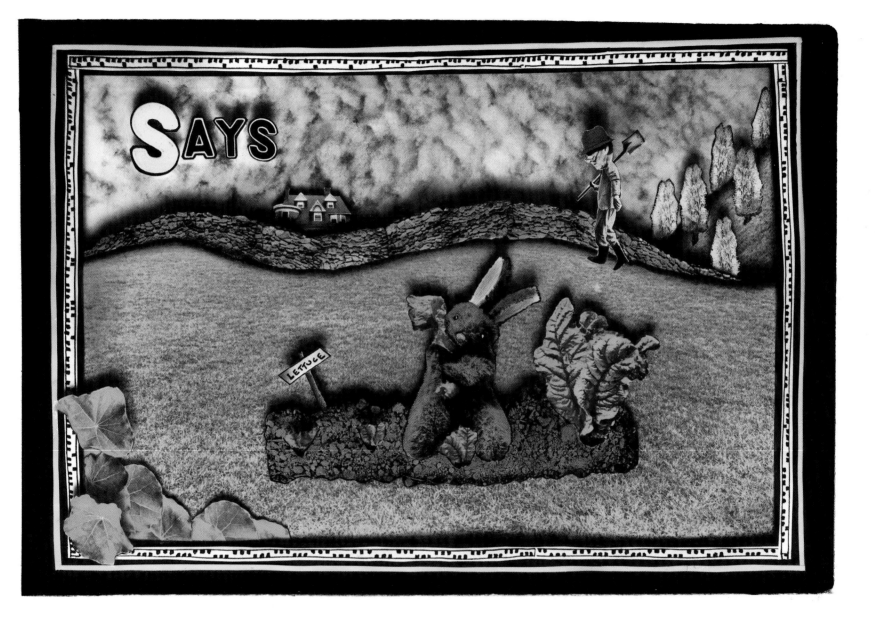

Author's Note

Why not try to make up some alphabet sentences of your own? You can make up three-word sentences, four-word sentences, eight-word sentences, or more. Some of these sentences may be pretty silly, but that's part of the fun. If you want, you can put on a play acting out your alphabet sentences, as the characters do in this book, or you can write your own book.

Here's one way I make up alphabet sentences. First I write the letters at the top of the page. Then I think of all the words I know that start with each letter, and put them under the correct heading, like this:

A	B	C	D	E
all	babies	can	dump	elephants
after	beautiful	cartoons	deer	equal
armadillo	butterfly	castle	drink	ear

(The dictionary is a big help in this game.) Then I start combining words and see what sentences I can come up with. I wonder what *you* will come up with.   *Karen Born Andersen*

A Note About the Art

The art for this book consists of hand-colored photocollage. The cut-out elements of each collage were arranged on two or more planes of suspended glass. The structure, lit to cast shadows creating a three-dimensional effect, was then photographed.

2/12/03

For Flint K.B.A.   o   *For Karen* F.B.

Published by Dial Books / A Division of Penguin Books USA Inc.
375 Hudson Street / New York, New York 10014

Text copyright © 1993 by Karen Born Andersen
Pictures copyright © 1993 by Flint Born
All rights reserved / Printed in Hong Kong by South China Printing Company (1988) Limited
First Edition
1 3 5 7 9 10 8 6 4 2

Library of Congress Cataloging in Publication Data
Andersen, Karen Born.
An alphabet in five acts / by Karen Born Andersen ; pictures by Flint Born.— 1st ed. p.   cm.
Summary: Five illustrated sentences present the alphabet, with one word representing each letter in turn.
ISBN 0-8037-1440-8 (trade).—ISBN 0-8037-1441-6 (lib.)   1. English language—Alphabet—Juvenile literature.
[1. Alphabet.]   I. Born, Flint, ill.   II. Title.   PE1155.A49 1993   421′.1—dc20   [E]   92-26947   CIP   AC